The Best Book of Whales and Dolphins

Christiane Gunzi

KINGFISHER

NEW YORK

Contents

4 Meet the whales

6 The first whales

Created for Kingfisher Publications Plc
by Picthall & Gunzi Limited

Author and editor: Christiane Gunzi
Designer: Dominic Zwemmer
Editorial assistance: Lauren Robertson
Illustrators: Michael Langham Rowe,
 William Oliver, Jim Channell
Consultants: Julie Childs and
 Theresa Greenaway

KINGFISHER
Larousse Kingfisher Chambers Inc.
80 Maiden Lane
New York, New York 10038
www.kingfisherpub.com

First published in 2001
10 9 8 7 6 5 4 3 2 1

1TR/0401/WKT/MAR/128KMA

Copyright © Kingfisher Publications Plc 2001

All rights reserved under
International and Pan-American Copyright Conventions

LIBRARY OF CONGRESS CATALOGING-IN-PUBLICATION DATA
has been applied for.

ISBN 0-7534-5369-X

Printed in Hong Kong

14 Blowholes

16 Hunting for prey

24 Water babies

26 Whales in danger

Meet the whales

Whales are the largest sea creatures on Earth, and the blue whale is the biggest animal ever known. Whales are divided into two groups. Toothed whales include dolphins and porpoises, and baleen whales include blue whales and humpbacks. Whales are mammals, and they are found in every ocean. Some have lived for up to 200 years!

An adult blue whale measures up to 85 feet in length, and can weigh up to 100 tons.

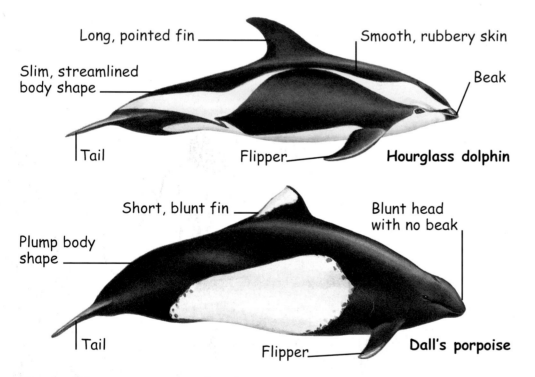

Long, pointed fin

Smooth, rubbery skin

Slim, streamlined body shape

Beak

Tail

Flipper

Hourglass dolphin

Short, blunt fin

Blunt head with no beak

Plump body shape

Tail

Flipper

Dall's porpoise

Dolphin or porpoise?

Porpoises and dolphins are much smaller than whales. A dolphin has a slim body with pointed fins. It also has a beak. A porpoise has no beak, and it is plumper than a dolphin. Its fins are short and more blunt. One kind of porpoise has no fins at all.

A blue whale calf drinks 158 gallons of its mother's milk every day for seven months before it begins to eat other food.

4

Gentlest of giants

Blue whales spend the summers in the
Arctic and Antarctic oceans, where
there is plenty of krill and plankton
to eat. In the winter, these whales
travel to warm waters to breed.
Females give birth to one baby every
two or three years. A newborn calf
usually weighs over three tons!

The first whales

About 55 million years ago, some of the mammals that lived on land moved to live in the sea. They may have been looking for food there. Over millions of years, these mammals gradually adapted (became suited) to living underwater, and slowly evolved into the first kinds of whales. Two of the earliest whales were Basilosaurus and Durodon. Basilosaurus was as big as a sperm whale!

Sea monster

Basilosaurus lived between 38 and 45 million years ago, and Durodon lived 25 million years ago. Basilosaurus was about 75 feet long and weighed at least five tons. This carnivore hunted other sea creatures.

Basilosaurus

Basilosaurus had big teeth for catching other sea creatures.

Durodon

Basilosaurus's skull

Nostril near front of head

Old and new

The teeth of the first whales, such as Basilosaurus, were a mixture of sizes and shapes. But a modern whale, such as the killer whale, has teeth that are all alike. Ancient whales had nostrils near the front of the head, but whales today have nostrils much farther back. These nostrils are the whale's blowholes.

Killer whale's skull

Teeth different sizes and shapes

Nostril far back on head

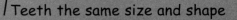
Teeth the same size and shape

7

A world of whales

There are about 11 different kinds of baleen whales and 67 kinds of toothed whales, including dolphins and porpoises. Some whales, such as the blue whale and the humpback, are enormous—others are very small. The pygmy sperm whale is one of the smallest. Its blunt head is the same shape as a shark's. The narwhal is one of the most unusual. The male has a long tusk on the front of its head that makes it look like a unicorn.

Sowerby's beaked whale
(at least 18 ft. long)

Bottlenose whale
(up to 32 ft. long)

Whale camouflage

The color of a whale helps it blend in with its surroundings. Most whales are blue-gray, to match the sea. Belugas are white, and narwhals are mottled black and white. This helps camouflage them in their icy Arctic home.

Beluga (or white) whale
(up to 18 ft. long)

Sei whale
(up to 62 ft. long)

Minke whale
(up to 33 ft. long)

Narwhal
(up to 15.5 ft. long)

8

False killer whale
(up to 19.5 ft. long)

Pygmy sperm whale
(up to 11 ft. long)

Killer whale
(up to 31 ft. long)

Humpback whale
(up to 53 ft. long)

Cuvier's beaked whale
(up to 24.5 ft. long)

Long-finned
pilot whale
(up to 20 ft. long)

Northern right whale
(up to 59 ft. long)

A world of dolphins

There are more than 30 kinds of dolphins and six kinds of porpoises. Most dolphins live in the ocean. Some dolphins live in rivers, so they are known as freshwater or river dolphins. Porpoises usually live in small groups near the coast. Dolphins and porpoises are closely related, but they belong to separate families and are different in shape.

Indus river dolphin
(up to 8 ft. long)

Unusual dolphins

River dolphins have extremely long beaks and tiny eyes, and some of them can hardly see at all. They are usually gray or creamy-white in color, but some are completely pink!

Bottlenose dolphin
(up to 13 ft. long)

Common dolphin
(up to 8.5 ft. long)

Risso's dolphin
(at least 13 ft. long)

Atlantic hump-backed
dolphin (up to 9 ft. long)

Harbor porpoise
(up to 6 ft. long)

Finless porpoise
(up to 6 ft. long)

Burmeister's porpoise
(up to 6.5 ft. long)

Spectacled porpoise
(at least 7.5 ft. long)

Gulf of California
porpoise (up to 5 ft. long)

Dall's porpoise
(up to 7.5 ft. long)

Striped dolphin
(up to 9 ft. long)

Rough-toothed dolphin
(up to 8 ft. long)

White-beaked dolphin
(up to 10 ft. long)

Atlantic white-sided dolphin
(up to 9 ft. long)

11

Life in the oceans

Most whales, dolphins, and porpoises live in the open ocean, and they are superb swimmers.

Some of the largest animals spend some of their time alone, but whales, dolphins, and porpoises usually live in groups. Large groups are called herds, and there can be thousands of dolphins in a single herd. All whales are very acrobatic and often leap right out of the water.

Southern right whale breaching

Breaching whale

When whales rise up out of the water then fall onto their backs with a huge splash, it is called breaching. Nobody is sure why whales breach. Perhaps they do it just for fun!

Barnacles, lice, and worms live on this whale's head in lumps called bonnets.

Southern right whale dolphins porpoising

Leaping dolphins

Dolphins are playful creatures. They enjoy racing through the water and jumping high into the air. When they leap out of the water in a curve, it is called porpoising. Dolphins do this more often than porpoises!

13

Blowholes

A whale or dolphin breathes through a blowhole on top of its head. A baleen whale has two blowholes, and a toothed whale has one. The blowholes can open when the whale swims to the surface for air, and close again when it goes back underwater. Some sperm whales can hold their breath underwater for two hours or more.

Two blowholes produce two spouts of vapor

Northern right whales

Spout of vapor is low

Bowhead whales

Spout of vapor points to the left

Sperm whale

Spout shapes

The spout coming out of the blowhole is the whale's warm breath, which contains water vapor. Vapor is a mist that is made when the whale's breath mixes with cold air. Scientists recognize whales by the shape of their spouts.

Spout of vapor is large and spread out

Fin whales

14

A sperm whale flicks up its tail as it dives down to catch fish and squid on the seabed.

Deepest diver

The sperm whale is the largest toothed whale. It can measure up to 65 feet long. Sperm whales can dive deeper than any other sea mammal, reaching depths of 10,000 feet or more. When a sperm whale swims to the surface to blow air out of its blowhole, there is a large cloud of vapor and a thunderous sound like an explosion!

Hunting for prey

The killer whale, or orca, is the only kind of whale that **hunts other sea mammals.**

It has sharp, cone-shaped teeth for grabbing prey. Killer whales eat seals and dolphins and sometimes attack other whales. Dolphins, porpoises, sperm whales, and pilot whales are also toothed whales. They hunt fish and squid and usually swallow their food whole.

Killer whale

Teamwork

Killer whales work in teams to catch their prey, and then they share their meal. They usually hunt for seals swimming near the seashore. Sometimes a killer whale will almost swim onto the beach to grab a seal.

A killer whale's mouth opens wide when it tries to catch its prey.

16

What toothed whales eat

Most toothed whales feed mainly on fish, squid, and octopus. Some whales also eat shrimp and other crustaceans. Killer whales sometimes catch seabirds and turtles!

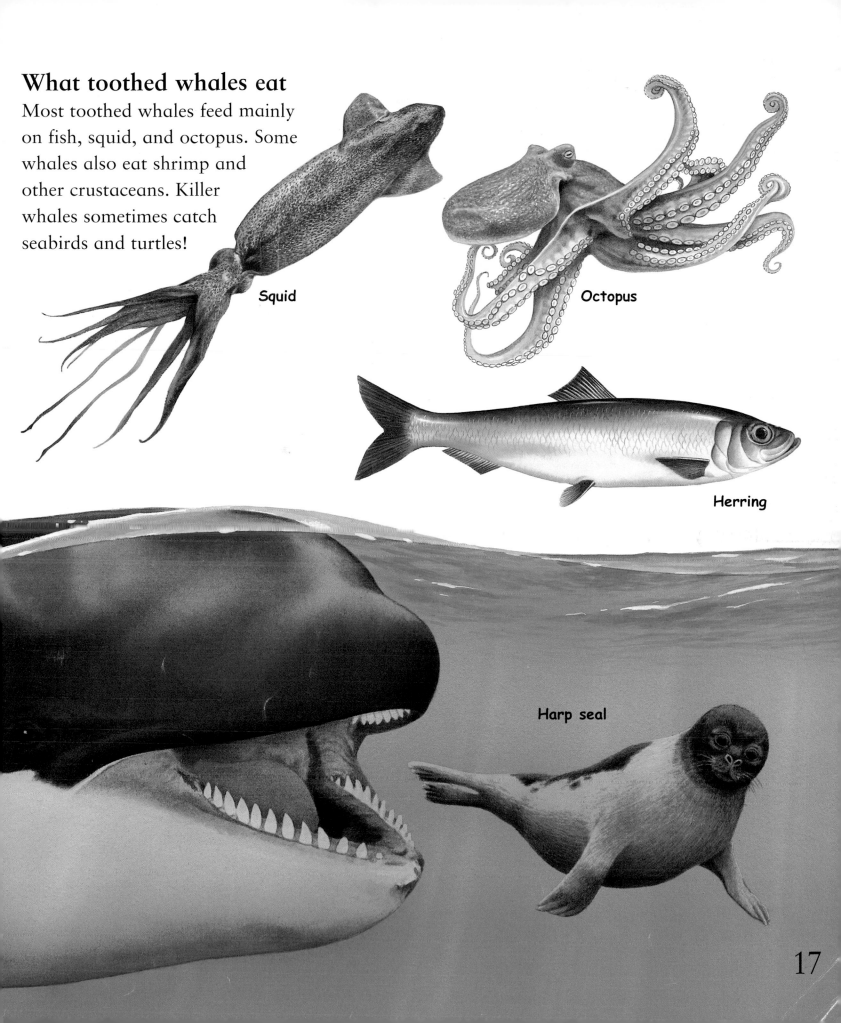

Squid

Octopus

Herring

Harp seal

17

Filtering food

Humpback whales catch their food using their baleen. Baleen, or whalebone, are the long, hair-lined plates inside a baleen whale's mouth. They help the whale to catch prey. As the whale swims forward, water filters through its open mouth. When the whale closes its mouth, the water is forced out, and tiny creatures are trapped inside the baleen. Humpbacks also catch food by blowing out long clouds of bubbles. This is called bubble netting.

A humpback swims up inside its bubble net to feed on krill that is trapped at the surface.

An adult krill measures up to 2 inches in length

What baleen whales eat

Baleen whales feed mostly on krill and plankton, which they trap with their baleen. Krill are crustaceans that look like shrimp. A humpback whale eats tons of krill every day.

Bubble netting

A humpback whale swims up to the surface in a spiral, blowing air out of its blowhole. The bubbles rise up like a string of beads and trap krill inside a "net." The whale then surfaces and eats its meal.

A humpback has up to 400 hairy baleen plates in its mouth

Throat groove

Baleen

Trapping food

As a humpback gulps in water and food, the grooves on its throat stretch so that it can catch more food. The water is squeezed out of its mouth through the baleen plates, but the food is trapped.

Talking underwater

Dolphins use whistles, wails, clicks, and barks to talk to each other, to find their way, and to locate food. The clicking sounds that they make travel through the water and bounce off objects, sending back echoes. This is called echolocation, and dolphins use it to find prey. Baleen whales do not use echolocation to find food, but the sounds that they make are probably the loudest in the animal kingdom. Whale songs travel many miles underwater.

False killer whale lob tailing

Lob tailing

Sometimes whales splash their tails on the surface of the water to show other whales where they are. This is called lob tailing.

When a dolphin whistles loudly to its companions, bubbles may come out of the blowhole on its head

Atlantic spotted dolphins

Dolphin speak

Dolphins sometimes squawk at each other when they are quarreling. A dolphin can open its mouth underwater without choking because it uses the blowhole for breathing, and not its mouth.

Jaw clapping

Whales sometimes poke their heads out of the water and snap their jaws shut loudly to warn others to stay away. This is called jaw clapping.

Long-finned pilot whale jaw clapping

Every dolphin makes its own whistling sound

Chatty whale

The beluga is nicknamed the "singing whale" and the "sea canary" because it makes so many different sounds. The beluga also makes faces, probably as a signal to others. Scientists are not sure what these expressions mean.

The beluga is the only whale that can change the shape of its lips.

When the mouth curls up, it looks as if the whale is smiling.

The fatty lump on the beluga's head can change shape too.

When the lump is big, the beluga is signaling other whales.

21

Dancing dolphins

 **Dusky dolphins are friendly and playful.** They enjoy swimming alongside boats and leaping high into the air. These dolphins live in family groups, and several groups may join up to form a herd. Dusky dolphins feed on all kinds of prey, including squid and deep-sea fish.

Dusky dolphin somersaulting in midair

Acrobats of the ocean

Dusky dolphins are probably the most acrobatic of all the dolphins. They can leap up to 17 feet into the air to do a somersault, then land on their backs with a big splash.

Herd of dusky dolphins racing a tourist boat

22

Happy families

The killer whale is also called the orca. These creatures live in every ocean, especially the cold Arctic and Antarctic oceans. Orcas live and hunt together in family groups called pods. There can be up to 55 animals in one pod. The chief male has a fin on its back that can be almost 6.5 feet tall!

Young killer whales stay close to their mothers for several years

23

Water babies

 Whales and dolphins give birth underwater, and their young are able to swim right away.

A baby dolphin or whale is called a calf. A bottlenose dolphin calf is about 3 feet long when it is born, and its fins are bendy. The calf feeds on its mother's milk for many months before it begins to catch its own food. The mother teaches and protects her calf for nearly two years.

The gray whale's trail

Every year gray whales swim thousands of miles to breed and to feed. This is called migration. At two months old a calf must swim 6,200 miles with its mother.

1 While the baby dolphin is being born, another female, called an "aunt," helps the mother and protects her from sharks.

An adult female helps protect a mother and baby.

Bottlenose dolphin giving birth

2 The baby dolphin is born in shallow water near the surface. Dolphins and whales are always born tail first.

Gray whale migration

In the summer gray whales feed in the cold waters off the coast of Alaska.

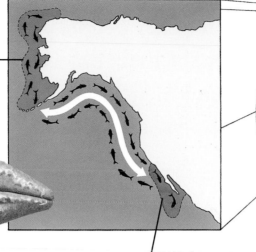

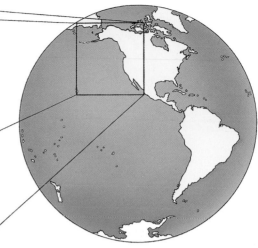

A mother and baby swim up the coast together, close to the shore.

In the winter females give birth in the warm waters off the coast of California.

The gray whale's migration is up and down the western coast of North America

The mother stays near the surface during the birth

3 The newborn calf has no air in its lungs, so it sinks at first. But its mother will quickly guide it to the surface to take its first breath of air.

A dolphin calf can swim well as soon as it is born

Whales in danger

For hundreds of years people hunted whales for their baleen, blubber, oil, and meat. Today whales and dolphins are still in danger. Many are trapped in fishing nets and drown. Others are killed by pollution when oil leaks from ships. Sometimes a herd becomes stranded on the shore and cannot get back to the sea. When this happens, people try to make the whales comfortable until the tide comes in again.

Stranded pilot whales

A whale cannot breathe on land because its heavy body squashes its lungs, so the animal must be returned to the water as quickly as possible. People can help by keeping whales wet with seawater so that their skin does not dry out. Water must never go inside the blowhole.

Helpers protect pilot whales from the Sun with towels and seawater

Trapped in a net

When people fish for tuna, they often catch dolphins by mistake. Dolphins become trapped in the nets when they chase the fish. In some countries people now catch tuna with a rod and line instead of a net. Tuna that is caught this way is called "dolphin-friendly" tuna.

Dolphin and tuna caught in a net

The label on a can of tuna will tell you if the fish was caught with a rod and line.

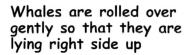

Whales are rolled over gently so that they are lying right side up

Dolphins and us

People have been fascinated by dolphins for thousands of years. There are stories of dolphins saving people from drowning and helping fishermen catch fish. Some of these tales are true! Dolphins are smart, playful creatures that enjoy swimming with humans. They often look as if they are smiling, which is possibly why we like them so much.

Children meeting a friendly Hector's dolphin

Meeting dolphins

Hector's dolphins are not at all shy, and they will approach beaches to play with swimmers, especially children! When people swim with dolphins, they should not touch them on the head.

All in a spin

Spinner dolphins are so named because they often leap out of the water and spin around and around. They can spin around as many as seven times before falling back into the water!

Diver with group of wild spinner dolphins

Studying whales

You can see whales and dolphins in every ocean of the world. In some countries people go whale watching on boats. By studying these majestic creatures in their natural home, scientists are able to learn how they feed and breed, and can help them to survive in the wild.

Every humpback's tail looks different.

Each tail has its own markings.

Whale spotting

When a whale dives, it flicks its tail out of the water. Scientists can recognize a humpback whale by its tail—each one is different.

Tagging dolphins

Scientists put tags on some kinds of dolphins. The tags send out signals for the scientists to follow, which helps them discover how these animals behave in the wild.

Bottlenose dolphins with special tags on their fins

Scientists watching Keiko from a distance

Free at last

Keiko the whale was the star of a film about a captive killer whale that was set free. In real life Keiko lived in a small, shallow tank in an aquarium. Thousands of children wrote letters to ask for Keiko to be freed, so now he is being returned to the wild!

Keiko swimming in the Arctic Ocean

Glossary

baleen The long, hairy plates inside the mouths of baleen whales. Baleen works like a sieve to trap tiny sea creatures, and it can grow to over 13 ft. long.

blubber The thick layer of fat beneath the skin of a whale or dolphin that keeps it warm.

breaching When a whale or dolphin rises up out of the water and falls back down with a big splash.

calf A baby whale, dolphin, cow, or elephant.

camouflage The coloring that helps a whale blend in with its surroundings.

captive A captive animal is one that does not live in the wild. Captive whales and dolphins usually live in aquariums.

carnivores Animals that kill and eat other animals.

crustaceans Animals such as crabs and shrimp.

echolocation How toothed whales find their way and find food. They send out sounds that bounce off objects and come

back to them as echoes. These tell them how far away an object is.

evolve To develop gradually. Animals and plants have evolved over millions of years.

extinct When a type of animal no longer lives on Earth it is extinct. Basilosaurus is extinct.

herd A large group of mammals that live together. Whales, dolphins, cattle, and elephants live in herds.

krill Shrimplike crustaceans that live in huge swarms in the southern oceans.

mammal A warm-blooded animal, such as a whale, that feeds its young on milk.

migration The movement of animals, such as whales, from

one area to another. Whales migrate to find food and to breed.

plankton Tiny creatures and plants that live in the sea.

pod A group of related whales or dolphins.

porpoising The movement of dolphins as they leap out of the water in an arc.

predator An animal that hunts other animals. A killer whale is known as a predator because it hunts dolphins and seals.

prey Any creature that is killed and eaten by another animal.

stranding When whales or dolphins are stuck, or stranded, on a beach.

tusk An animal's tooth that grows very long. Male narwhals have one tusk.

whaling Hunting whales for their oil, blubber, and baleen—also known as whalebone.

Index